Reboot and Rejoice

*How I healed from Parkinson's Disease
using the body/mind practice of qigong*

Regimen, background and personal reflections

BIANCA MOLLÉ, M.ED.

METTAMORPHIX PRESS

2013

Reboot & Rejoice: How I Healed from Parkinson's Disease Using the Body/Mind Practice of Qigong: Regimen, Background, and Personal Reflections

Copyright © 2013 by Bianca Mollé

Mettamorphix Press
www.mettamorphix.com
SECOND PRINTING

cover design by Nelson Salis
www.nelsonsalis.com
production by Isaiah Singer
www.isaiahsinger.com

"The purpose of healing is not to be forever happy; that is impossible. The purpose of healing is to live while you are alive instead of dying while you are alive. Healing is about being broken and whole at the same time."

- Geneen Roth

Table of Contents

Author's Note

The chapters with both initial quotes and "Afterthoughts" are revised editions of original blog postings. I reread online blogs and added thoughts or experiences from myself and others that occurred after posting. The initial quotes, I believe, help sum up the energy or message of the piece. I have always enjoyed reading books that provided this additional element, and it is my sincere hope that you will, too.

At the end of this work is an Appendix which includes authors, books, poems, websites and any other materials either mentioned directly here, or that I think may prove helpful to anyone interested in exploring this type of healing in more depth.

There is now a DVD available to support this book. *One Stop Shopping for Healing* can be found at www.mettamorphix.com.

Caveat: please consult with a medical professional before attempting to change dosages; major damage can occur when there is a cavalier attitude about drug administration.

Preface/Mission Statement

This endeavor is an attempt to share the internal process of my healing from Parkinson's Disease as well as what I have learned from it since then. I am not the first kid on the block to undergo this experience. People such as John Coleman, Janice Walton-Hadlock, and Howard Shifke share recovery stories from not only personal perspective, but also from the wisdom of various vantage points of their own histories and expertise with alternative methods.

When I began my healing journey, I had heard of none of these role models or methods. The self-description that best applies here is that I was an "energy bonehead." In fact, I had run across energetic healing once or twice in searching for comfort for my autistic son, but I didn't realize that's what was happening. We had reached the end of the road with any assistance conventional therapies could offer, so we moved on to explore avenues like Auditory Integration Training and Sensory Integration Training. Both therapies greatly upgraded

Justin's level of functioning. In retrospect, I now see that they had vibrational level and energy movement in common with qigong, the mode of alternative healing that brought me back to myself.

I have had to sit long and hard with myself to determine, considering the wisdom and information of those who walk before me, whether I had anything of further value to offer. Old insecurities arose as I deliberated whether or not sharing my own story would be redundant in a field where those far more knowledgeable in the ways of healing had recovered prior to myself. It was in a recent meeting with my IT person and co-editor, Isaiah Singer, that my purpose was suggested.

Isaiah is my son Aaron's friend from high school days. He made the journey from Berkeley to Dartmouth to join us for Aaron's graduation in 1997, and served as best man when Kathy and Aaron were married in 2002. He is aware of our family story. When I shared with him my reluctance to move forward with this project, Isaiah suggested that what makes it interesting and, more importantly, useful, is my role as "skeptic." I'm not sure "skeptic" is the exact term that applies, as desperation often brings with it a willingness to believe, a "why not?" attitude. This is where I was when I began practicing Wisdom Healing (Zhineng, Chi-lel) Qi-gong.

So perhaps my story can help persuade those who, like myself, have had little to no prior experience with how energy works, and who approach with hesitance the idea of fixing the body through empowering the mind. Self-forgiveness, I found, must be included in the process. "If somehow my mind, and redirecting it, can make me better, did my mind have a role in bringing about the condition I am trying to heal? Can I forgive myself without blaming myself? Can I realize that I was always doing what I thought was my best simply because I did not see another way? Finally, can I love myself and realize that self-love does not involve the negative associations of egoism?" These are questions that I know were in my psyche, but which only materialized to articulate form as a result of the healing process.

It is my hope that this is one way I can help assist almost-skeptics and encourage them to go forward in the process of returning to health. If you are sitting with any chronic health condition, concerned with further deterioration, looking to move away from the palliative suggestions of traditional medicine and desiring to move on to working with, and then gradually eliminating, the cause of what ails you, this is for you. May you derive some benefit from these pages and create your own version of a healing story. There can never be too many. Haola! (All is well, so be it.)

A Word About Terminology

I am sometimes asked if I refer to what happened to me as "healing" or "recovery" or "cure." Wanting to get the terminology right, I consulted my *American Heritage Dictionary of the English Language*, Fourth Edition (over 2068 pages). This lexicon actually held all three terms synonymous.

It seems that we ourselves use the term "cure" most often in the medical sense, and it seems to connote a disappearance of all symptoms. Healing and recovery have more of a body/mind connotation. A healing can include a spiritual component. An alcoholic can be "in recovery."

So the latter two terms, healing and recovery, imply some work being done by the affected individual, therefore I use them interchangeably. I view my experience with Parkinson's as a continuum. The precursors could have begun in childhood or early adulthood. After diagnosis, once I became aware that this condition was not merely one of tremor, I realized many of the symptoms had been with me for many years. Happily, they exist no more. But I am still working on their forerunners, leg and foot issues, and others not in the physical realm.

These challenges are in great part what this book addresses. As you work on your recovery from chronic illness, I am giving a heads-up on what may lie ahead.

1
Gratitude/Gratefulness

"Let us be grateful to the people who make us happy; they are the charming gardeners who make our souls blossom."

- Marcel Proust

Many books include a section for acknowledgements. I feel it is important to take this one step further and demonstrate, from the get-go, the importance of gratitude to healing, and in general, to improve one's outlook on life. This raises vibrational level, which, when high enough, promotes healing.

My skeptical self probably would have stopped right here. Vibrations are not visible, but neither is sound, wind, electricity and so many other powerful forces in our universe. My first qigong lesson taught me that 96% of the universe is unseen. The material world we live in comprises only 4% of what exists. Diagnoses and prognoses are made within that 4%.

I invite you to jump outside the box with me, and in so doing perhaps increase the odds by 96%.

There seems to be some hair-splitting about gratitude vs. gratefulness. For the purposes of this publication, and in the interest of expedient clarity, I use them synonymously.

In my passion to better understand the course of my full recovery from Parkinson's Disease, I find I owe a universe of thanks to the universe and every particle within it. Anything living now, before, or to come has had a part in paving my path, one that I now attempt to map for others.

To narrow it down a bit, I am grateful to all qigong practitioners and energy workers, particularly to Mingtong Gu and his mentor, Dr. Pang Ming. I give loving thanks to Teacher Ma and Teacher Zhao, my angels in China, who taught me, beyond the physical practice, the love that binds together the body and mind. This they had me learn from some higher plane, as we shared no common spoken language. Much gratitude also to Linling Xie, and to Teacher Zheng, an earnest young man and gentle, powerful teacher/healer.

I must also here remember Teacher Wu and the other wonderful teachers and community members at the Community Center in Guelin where we practiced qigong several hours each day for two weeks. Their generosity of spirit and willingness and enthusiasm to incorporate "us" into their group made me feel welcome in a land that I now choose to regard as my second home. The "us" of whom I speak and to whom I am also grateful is the American group that followed Mingtong and his wife, Linling, to Guelin, China, for an intensive healing retreat. About twenty-five of us co-existed for several weeks, each of us working on our own health and recovery.

Thank you also to "Auntie", Linling's relative, who noticed the pain I was trying to hide one day and almost forcibly invited me into her room (we had no common language), where she pounded my muscles into silence and submission in the most necessary, awesome, and unsolicited massage. Haola!

Catherine and Steve, I'll never forget your wonderful parting gift, a dramatic satire of our experiences, bursting with talent, creativity, and humor. Laughter is indeed the best medicine. Elizabeth, thank you for being my travel buddy, which often amounted to caretaker, when the leg pain forced me to sit, and the foggy brain would have sent me to Seoul instead of Hong Kong. Speaking of Hong Kong, thank you for planning and orchestrating our daytrip to the Po Lin Monastery, another unforgettable experience.

Further into recovery, my curiosity led me to read omnivorously about chi, meditative practice, body-mind-spiritual-connection, the brain and neurology. Some author names that come to mind here are: Pema Chodrun, Duane Elgin, David R. Hawkins, Rudy Tanzi and Deepak Chopra, Eben Alexander III, MD, Roger Jahnke, Greg Braden, Bruce Lipton, Joe Dispenza, Janice Walton-Hadlock, John Coleman, Amit Goswami, Thich Nhat Hanh, Lao-tsu and all poets. Thanks to these writers for their insight and inspiration. A list of titles and authors will be presented in the appendix of this book.

Thanks also to every student I've ever "taught" and to every client I've ever coached or served. The receiving is, of course, within the giving. Thanks to my lifelong community of personal friends and colleagues, we teach and learn from each other continually. Thanks to the Spirit Rock Community, for providing a spiritual sanctuary and ongoing stimulation.

A universe of gratitude to my friend, Jean Adams, for convincing me to attend my first "Healer Within" workshop by relating the story of a friend who used qigong to help heal from cancer.

To Lilou Mace of "Juicy Living Tours," for her interest in sharing my story. To Dr. Robert Rogers, who picked up the ball from there and became an unwitting mentor to a sometimes unwilling mentee.

To my brother, Hank, personal and professional hero (retired NYC fireman and first responder to 9-11), I thank you for your under-standing and support. I'll always remember the family time you arranged for us in Orlando, Florida, with Aimee, Kyle, and Adrianna. And thank you for being the one shoulder I felt I could cry on when putting on the brave face everywhere else.

To my son Aaron, firstborn child and gift of the universe, for his cool and abiding intellect and support, child-like humor, enduring patience and compassion. And thanks also to you and Kat for providing me with cuddly, sassy, immortality in the form of Emma and Alex.

To my son Justin, who ranks up there with Parkinson's as my most challenging teacher, I thank you for presenting your autism as just one small part of who you are. Your spirit has always shown through and guided me to advocate for you, and in so doing, when the time came, for myself. Unconditional love is indeed the answer.

To Isaiah Singer, IT person extraordinaire, and more: for intelligence, interest, and support.

To Nelson Salis, who managed to take the collage of forms and colors inside my head and conceptualize images to which I could respond with a resounding "Yes!"

To those of you now turning these pages, I

thank you for providing me with purpose. As I awaken from the slumber of poor health and rub the sleep from my eyes, myself and others like me gently nudge those beside us: Arise, awake. It is a new day. Come discover yourself and the beauty that lies within. You are loved. Haola! (All is well. So be it.)

2
Caveat

"Take someone who doesn't keep score, who's not looking to be richer, or afraid of losing . . . he's free."

– Rumi

Again and again, I am approached by those who want a step-by-step account of my recovery. Over and over I find ways to sidestep this request, not an easy task for someone who enjoys, even prides herself on direct and clear expression. Before you turn away in frustration, please hear me out. I do this for you, out of respect to the individual healing process. We humans too often place ourselves unnecessarily in competitive situations. It's great to get the adrenalin flowing for a triathlon or for a stage performance, or speaking engagement, not for healing.

Healing is not a linear process. Healing is about

relaxing so one can be openly receptive to the required energies. Few reading this now share my specific DNA or anatomical structure, not to mention all the non-material components that make me who I am and you yourself. Healing energy may, and often will, apply itself differently for you. Attempting to follow me without allowing room for the uniqueness that is you invites difficulty.

When I instructed 6th graders in Introductory Art, soon after I gave an assignment, someone would complain: "So-and-so is copying me." I would explain how that really wasn't so, as each of us would execute the same ideas differently. We all learn to write the same letters of the alphabet, yet everyone's penmanship is unique. Please allow your healing to express itself naturally, don't attempt to manipulate or redirect it. Just let it happen as it may. Heal your way, not mine. Along the way there are bound to be similarities, and the information presented in the following pages will give an account of my reflections on the process.

"Perfectionism is self-abuse of the highest order."

– Anna Wilson Scheaf

Here I must also mention another human trait, perhaps sometimes helpful, but not for healing purposes: perfectionism. When watching instructional DVDs or working with meditational CDs, you are not relaxing if you are beating yourself up about imperfect form or distracted thought. Instead congratulate yourself for doing the practice, and for returning to it, day after day, even if you don't look or sound exactly like the featured instructor. Healing is about intention, not perfection.

I exemplify that. My pronated ankles and duckfooted stance make me a less than wonderful visual example, yet that didn't stop my recovery. Also, at the time I began doing the sound healing meditational chants, there were no phonetic charts available. I made the sounds as best I could, sometimes, in my head, silently whispering: "What he said" along with my verbal attempt at butchered Chinese. I healed anyway. Why? Two words: Intent and Dedication. I practiced three hours a day, every day, minimum. I loved having a purpose and began to believe I could make a difference for myself. And the frequent repetition was re-training my brain so I could get my life back.

So go ahead and read further, keeping in mind that you are the one healing yourself. I, along with others like myself, am providing you with community, a connectedness necessary for one to thrive. Take off your shoes, get comfortable. Recovery is possible.

"Throw away holiness and wisdom. When some folks are called saints, other folks think of themselves as sinners. When one fellow is called wise, others imagine there is something they need to know. The Master doesn't have these categories; for her no one is wise or holy; thus, in her presence everyone feels at home."

> *- Tao Te Ching, translated by Stephen Mitchell*

I present my offering; it is hoped with the necessary humility and irreverence toward self.

3
Introducing Myself

"An autobiography usually reveals nothing bad about the writer except his memory."

- Marcel Proust

"All autobiography is self-indulgent."

- Daphne Du Maurier

The above quotes together summarize how I felt about sharing some of my early background. However, it was suggested by several people that some autobiography would be helpful in communicating my story of recovery. After all, I am not simply Parkinson's Disease, pre and post. Also, I noticed that when people have private sessions with me, they often ask autobiographical questions at the start and sometimes want to spend a bit of time there.

Perhaps this sharing elevates their comfort level and strengthens the personal connection, even though it makes me feel, as Du Maurier suggests, self-indulgent.

So here's a bit about me for those who may be interested. Feel free to skip to the next chapter. After all, this entire work is simply my recovery as told by me, and then my reflections on that. I must admit, that sounds pretty self-indulgent. However, it seems the most expedient way to share my message without posing as any type of expert.

My interest in spiritual life and the inner journey gradually ebbed as I made several discoveries early in life: there is no Santa, the Catholic clergy and its dogma are fallible, mothers can, and sometimes do, wither and succumb in their so-called prime. My prayers were not answered, and no one seemed interested in answering why not. We were all too busy trying to survive.

Life had its balance, however. There were sea-sprayed sojourns in Bermuda and in the Bahamas - I could feel the energy of the Caribbean throbbing under my sunburned feet.

There were romantic horseback rides along rugged trails in The Adirondack Mountains of upstate New York. There was the cultural potpourri offered by my native Empire State: theatre, museums, education, and all the colors and flavors of diversity before it became fashionable, and foremost, there was my own Italian heritage: heavy on pasta, opera, high expectations, and guilt.

I do not intend here to wade deeply into autobiography. My past is a place best enjoyed by a drive-by. As awe-ful, wonderful, and unique as those days were, I am not yet comfortable planning a lengthy visit. Perhaps that will occur as a manifestation of total healing, not only from Parkinson's, but from life itself - if such is possible.

More importantly, I believe my audience is most interested in the nitty gritty of how I managed full recovery from Parkinson's Disease. It is only from the perspective and insight gained from this, my current vantage point, 3 ½ years into recovery, that I understand that some biographical background is necessary to share. If the cause of this affliction were totally genetic or viral or organic, I could view myself as a number on a petri dish, pretty much the way I used to consider all disease. But my experience has taught me that as we root in early life, both our endurance and fragility are, to some degree, determined.

I grew up in a New York family that was Italian immigrant tough. My parents were first-generation Americans, born to parents struggling through the Great Depression in the Land of Opportunity. And they made it. They scrambled and sacrificed and enlisted their many children as labor force (maternal side). Or gained American citizenship and then escaped back to northern Italy where they, on the post-Depression American dollar, could live in villas and ship the kids out to religious-run boarding schools (paternal side). They returned to the states just in time to avoid the outbreak of WWII in Europe.

I was a Boomer baby, born at the end of the 1940's: my mother's firstborn, and the second child, first female, born to my father. I was not to learn of his first marriage, in the Catholic Church and quickly followed by divorce, or of the existence of a half-brother, only a few years my senior, till my sophomore year in college.

My mother, on a few occasions, had hinted there were some family secrets. For whatever reason, my usual curiosity was not aroused here. If an existential shrug can apply to a pre-teenager, that's more or less what I did. Not interested enough to ask, nor disinterested enough to forget.

The passion for learning was alive and well in most other areas, however. My college-educated mother, an anomaly for a woman in both her family and in our struggling middle-class neighborhood, had a steadfast little protégé in myself. A chalkboard desk, 78-speed record player, and numerous storybooks were my most valued possessions, and my mother taught me to read and write prior to entering school.

Her mini-lessons were virtually inhaled. My physical coordination and abilities were not commensurate to the intellectual gifts of childhood. I was the only kid in my kinder-garten class who could read or write her name, and the only one who could not tie her shoelaces or get a doorknob to turn in the right direction. Riding a two-wheeler sans training wheels did not occur till my eighth year, yet at barely six, under the tutelage of my Silesian Brothers-educated father, I was questioning the Latin grammar in the version of "Adeste Fideles" poor Sister Catherine Mary was teaching our first-grade class. Hopefully, I was only the messenger of hubris on that occasion. In my mind's eye, I can see my youthful, handsome father sporting a jaunty smirk.

From early childhood my mind was always far ahead of my body, and my way of coping was to ignore the body. But not always or altogether. The backyard swing set was a saving grace. I could hang out there and soar as high as the best of them, harmonizing with the arcs of trees and their beckoning branches. Also, my often tense and uncoordinated little body relaxed in the water. Here, my father was mentor, and I loved his attention so much that I actually regretted so quickly reaching the desired goal, since once I learned to swim, my dad returned to his adult endeavors.

So with a few notable and enjoyable exceptions, I began existing headfirst very early on. My body was often an unnecessary inconvenience I dragged along for the ride: excess baggage, so to speak. It took sixty years and Parkinson's

Disease for me to realize that life can only be lived to the fullest when body and mind unite, that this can best be accomplished through the mind-body disciplines, and that in the process, spirituality emerges as the authentic self begins to reappear. Today I continue to reap the benefits of this epiphany, not without wonder and not without pain. Feeling on all levels has returned, rendering me fully alive and completely vulnerable.

I do not mean to here discount all the physical conditions that contributed to the perfect storm that created Parkinson's in my body. I list here what I think may have been contributing causes, though in playing the role of Monday-morning quarterback, I realize this serves as mere speculation:

- I was a forceps baby, and the product of a very long labor.

- My early digestive system was extremely distressed and colicky.

- As a result I was given a formula of part soybean, part goat's milk (back then soy fields may have been heavily sprayed with insecticides).

- I was very left-handed and uncoordinated and had difficulty with physical directions and team sports.

- Flat feet, pronated arches and weak, tight hamstrings were evident early on, and my interest in wearing fashionable shoes made me stubbornly refuse to address correction.

- My ankles would not support ice-skating. I wore the adorable skirted outfit anyway!

- Prior to my 8th year, and shortly after the birth of my beloved brother, my mother's health began a rapid decline.

- I was primary caretaker to both of them, as my father often traveled with his work.

- When I was 17, my mother died from spinal cancer.

- On one occasion, in my twenties, I was scheduled for surgery for hammer toe and cancelled.

- In adulthood a Morton's neuroma appeared in my left foot, and after avoiding surgery for many years, I finally succumbed to the knife.

- As a result of years of leg/foot issues, the bones and connective tissue in my right leg have slid far inward to the left, at an angle. The knee, of course, followed.

- Since recovery from Parkinson's, I have been finally feeling the pain of prior conditions and addressing leg and foot issues, including the wearing of an orthopedic boot for several months.

- In adulthood I was diagnosed with anxiety, which I know I carried with me from my youth.

As the list progresses it becomes more and more difficult to winnow the physical from mental/ emotional, once again proving that we are a package deal. Our neurology, respiration, digestion all respond to the harmony or discord we experience within. Whether the chords we chose to play are major and upbeat, or minor and pessimistic, is up to us, and so often we don't know it. We continue to improvise riff after riff without the mindfulness that can be our salvation.

Parkinson's, for me, became the catalyst that urged me stop mindlessly humming a far-off tune, to pay attention and dance to my own harmony.

4

Did I Have to Go to China? An Energetic Turning Point

"Travellers, there is no path, paths are made by walking."

- Antonio Machado

Healing is an internal process that can happen anywhere. By the time I left for the retreat in Guelin my symptoms were already reversing: more energy, less tremor and sometimes less pain (sometimes more). I was clearly on my way to wellness, and so immersed in my daily practice and the exponential joy each day of recovery was bringing, that healing could have, and in all probability would have, continued anywhere. However, not the location of China itself, but the decision to go there, I feel, may have created a major energy shift that greatly contributed to my recovery.

It was mid-June in lovely Marin County, California, a location known worldwide for its beauty and ease of living. This was certainly not a place from which I needed to escape. Yet, here I was, seated in the auditorium of the Marin JCC, watching a slideshow orientation to the September-October Healing Intensive Retreat that was to take place in Guelin, China.

The photos were breathtaking: mossy karst cave formations lined snaking deep blue rivers, and wispy ethereal clouds beckoned from the sky like eternal fingers. Geography had never spoken like this to me before, or if it had, I hadn't been paying attention. The reaction was physical, a tugging at my heart. This physical feeling was familiar. In the past, when it related to giving something to myself, I could easily reject it. Not so this time. The dialogue in my head went something like this:

+Self: "This is so beautiful, and it's calling to me, almost like I've been here before and must return."

-Self: "That's just crazy. You have limited retirement funds and you had your big retirement trip just a few months ago when you visited friends in Australia. Besides, you're supposed to go to Tahoe in a few weeks with friends, and to have that long-coveted Yosemite stay with extended family and grandkids later this summer."

+Self: "I feel so strongly about this. The mystical beauty of the place reminds me of the film *Avatar*. I could cancel my other plans, possibly disappointing some other people, and go."

-Self: "There is supposed to be another China retreat in three years. I can save up and go then."

+Self: "I'm at this workshop because my Parkinson's is getting worse and I don't want to increase meds. Where will I be physically three years from now? What would it be like to travel then?"

-Self: "Only other people do things like this, not me."

+ Self: "This is my life, or what's left of it.

31

Maybe I should listen to myself. It's time for me to be like the other people who would go."

Without hesitation, knowing how I could talk myself out of it if I waited, I committed to the retreat and made the arrangements that weekend. Needless to say, those around me were astonished. I barely knew qigong or the people who were teaching it, yet I was going to spend three weeks in Guelin, practicing and deeply learning qigong from this couple along with their teacher contacts in China, some of whom had learned directly from Dr. Pang Ming, creator of Zhineng (Wisdom Healing) Qigong.

It took a big leap away from fear and toward self-empowerment for me to give myself this gift. Upon reflection, I notice that myself and other Persons With Parkinson's or with other chronic health challenges often find it much easier to be kind to others, to lavish family and friends with the time and attention one withholds from the self.

I sort of knew all this about myself before, but never really cared enough to change directions. This felt like a final bend in the road. Somewhere deep inside I knew that failure to act for myself this time could amount to a major difference. Besides, I had Parkinson's Disease - even the part of me that was worried about what others may think could dare them to challenge me on it. "Let the old retired schoolmarm indulge herself this one time." Haola!

5
Metamorphosis

"Just when the caterpillar thought the world was over, it became a butterfly"

- Proverb

I found a refrigerator magnet with that lovely proverb while waiting in line at Whole Foods shortly after I had been diagnosed with Parkinson's Disease. That saying became my mantra. I needed it to be my mantra because something told me that I could find some good in my situation. What was my situation?

For a number of years I had felt pain and extreme fatigue. Of course, I wasn't getting any younger, and teaching middle school requires so much energy in the classroom, and grading and planning in the 'off hours,' that I thought this was just a sign that I was ready to retire. And my handwriting had become so small and cramped that my students could no longer decipher the very cogent, insightful comments I ɹs making on their papers. Also, I had demonstrated a tremor that had gone from almost negligible to formidable over the past few years. When it got in the way of one of my favorite activities, eating, particularly eating soup, I went to see my first neurologist.

So, in April, 2008, after the usual questions and office observations of my physical condition, I was diagnosed with Parkinson's disease and began a program of treatment medications shortly after my retirement that June. I was taking Sinemet 25/100, the dopamine drug, three times a day, and Requip XL once daily.

After a while, my symptoms began to worsen. I had the option of increasing my meds, something I did not want to do. What I was really looking for was relief from the chronic pain. I could continually feel the muscles in my spine and arms and shoulders contract. Also, navigating stairs became a cumbersome endeavor, feeling like I had sandbags strapped to my arms and legs as I tried to make my way up to the bedroom.

Although I found myself increasingly inactive, it's not like I took my situation lying down. In the first year after my diagnosis I was proactive about research and treatment. I saw two neurologists and a movement disorder specialist, visited the Parkinson's Center in Sunnyvale, California, applied to and was selected for the PD DNA study co-sponsored by Sergei Brin of Google and Michael J. Fox, a study called "23andMe". I had also joined the local PD support group, researched and read numerous books and internet sites, practiced yoga till I became too stiff for "downward facing dog" and so off-balance that my tree pose looked like "downward falling tree"!! I had explored every avenue that resonated for me, visited everywhere, except inside myself.

Enter qigong, with its holistic approach that integrates the body, mind, and spirit.

In June of 2009, I attended a Healer Within workshop presented by Mingtong Gu at The Marin JCC. Mingtong explained a little bit about energy clearing out the blockages that cause disease and then we began a Level 1 physical practice, Lift Chi Up Pour Chi Down. Although I was shaky and had some difficulty following directions, I immediately felt a layer of pain lift away. Something was happening.

By the end of the weekend, Sunday night, I was convinced that qigong was working for me. Then, as we were leaving, Mingtong announced that anyone working on healing a chronic or serious illness should expect to practice a minimum of two to three hours daily. When I first heard this, my state shifted from blissful to annoyed. What? Two to three hours a day!! I didn't sign up for that!

The truth is, I hadn't signed up for Parkinson's either. So I began reflecting, and within a few moments my attitude changed from negative to positive. It was a no-brainer. What was better: two to three hours of qigong practice daily, or ten to twelve hours on the sofa each day, fatigued and in pain?

Probably one of the most difficult aspects of receiving my diagnosis was breaking the news to my family and friends. I couldn't bear to see sorrow or pity in their faces. So I told them that this was a gift. Here I was retiring, and now I had Carte Blanche to indulge myself. An example of this was visiting friends in Melbourne, Australia, during the winter of 2009.

Then, at the June qigong workshop, Mingtong offered a Zhineng qigong retreat in China for the following fall. I went home, got on the computer, and booked the trip to Guelin, which happens to be one of the most beautiful places on Earth. In retrospect I believe that my decision to "splurge" like this on myself, to listen to my inner voice that told me I should do this for myself, was a major energy shift in the right direction. It may have been one of the first aspects of my healing.

I began pinching myself. This Parkinson's journey was becoming a wonderful adventure. Qigong became my tour guide. I continued to practice at home, three hours a day, every day, doing the physical forms as well as the inner vibrational sound-healing meditation and other Zhineng (Wisdom Healing) qigong practices. Something unusual began to happen.

Generally, I didn't need the clock to tell me it was time for more PD meds, my body would tell me first. There would be increased tremor, stiffness and pain before the scheduled time for the next dose of dopamine. Then my body began forgetting. I took that as a sign that maybe I didn't need so much medication. So, very gradually, I reduced the drugs.

The day I left for the China retreat, I had been off all PD meds for almost a month. I wanted to work on my situation in Guelin without drugs possibly masking the symptoms. By this time much of the pain and fatigue had gone (there were also moments of heightened intensity), but not the tremors. This made meals in China, using chopsticks, an entertaining and suspenseful event. Needless to say, I managed to eat very well, despite some aborted efforts between rice bowl and final destination.

I continued my practice when I returned home from the retreat, and still practice a minimum of three hours a day, or minimum two hours a day when I'm working. (This retired teacher now substitutes and loves it, and is full of energy, not fatigue.) I saw the neurologist last week and was described as 'showing no signs of Parkinson's at all.' And it's not just me, some people with Parkinson's in the qigong community are demonstrating steady signs of improvement – like reduced tremors, better balance, increased flexibility in shoulders, faster, more fluid walking, and more energy.

If dedicated practice can show such benefits for a neurological condition, then what about for every human condition? Einstein said it best: "Either everything is a miracle or nothing is a miracle." We can create miracles in our lives through dedication, practice, and positive intention.

I came to qigong seeking a physical healing, and received that and so much more. Returning to the butterfly metaphor, I could say that qigong brought my body and spirit out of mothballs. And now that I'm flying free, let me wish one and all a giant "HAOLA" – "All is well."

Afterthoughts:

Because this was originally a timed oral presentation, I omitted some details like severe constipation, sometimes difficulty swallowing (choking sensation), sometimes dragging of right foot, Parkinson's dry eye, and some lack of mental clarity. Also, there was an occasional tremor of mouth/jaw. These descriptors, stacked atop each other, do not convey that there was very much a human being who still remained as active as possible whenever possible.

Also, my condition was not always or easily detectable. There were times when I was able to forget about it. I was making the best of my life, and in some ways perhaps allowing myself to begin to relax and give to myself, ironically, because I had a viable excuse!

Also, the text here cites three hours of daily formal practice. Currently, it's more like 1 ½ to 2 hours, with much time spent daily either talking or writing about qigong and healing. Love and gratitude were the big lessons I learned from all this and I try my best to practice this incessantly. Kindness holds a power all its own. As we practice this on ourselves, we become better able to share it with others.

6
My PD Recovery Regimen

"Your teacher can be the open door, but you must enter yourself."

– Lao Tzu

These are the materials I used (and still use, in combination with others) for my original healing from Parkinson's Disease. I will include prices for your convenience, but please be aware that I have no connection at all with the sales department at The Chi Center. Any shipping or ordering concerns need to be directed to the Chi Center staff.

I would like to share that in all my practices I employ my creative mind to visualize organs with energy flowing through them. For the brain I see Xmas lights twinkling back and forth, communicating with each other. Start from there and create your own powerful healing imagery. I will state here, and repeat later, that I practiced a minimum of 3 hours/day, and my clients doing the same are seeing results. Any amount of time spent in practice is helpful, so why not just go for it?

Chi Center Materials:

CDs:

- *Inner Vibrational Sound Healing* (single CD, $14.95) light blue color

- *Chi Healing Meditation* (Lachi), ($14.95) copper color

- *Awaken the Light Within* ($14.95) turquoise color

DVDs:

- *Qigong for Energy Healing (Lift Chi Up Pour Chi Down +3 Centers Merge: Standing Meditation)* ($24.95)

- There is a DVD called *Qigong for Internal Energy 1, Basic Practice* which has a number of the other physical qigong practices on it (lachi, wall squats, bow body, bending spines, chen chi, and even a bit of sound healing.). It's a wonderful tool, but if you are only going to purchase just one DVD, then I strongly recommend *Lift Chi Up, Pour Chi Down* as it really provides slow guided meditative movements. That's what started my recovery.

Books:

- *101 Miracles of Healing* by Luke Chan ($14.95)

- *Wisdom Healing Qigong* ($35.00) This book replaces the spiral bound manual I originally used, which is no longer available. This new version includes even more helpful information.

- I also read *The Living Universe* by Duane Elgin. It is no longer available on this site, and not directly a healing tool, but I found the explanations fascinating and helpful. You can probably find this on Amazon.

So, those are the starter materials I recommend.

Practice Regimen:

Think of this like "doses" of medication. Parkinson's requires a strong dose. I practiced 3 hours/day to see results.

Most days I did the DVD (*LCUPCD and Standing Meditation*) 3 times a day (120 min);

Plus *Sound Healing* CD (40 min)

1 time a day;

Plus *Awaken the Light Within* CD (40 min) at bedtime, in the middle of the night (if I awoke) and upon awakening, if I had time to linger in bed. It is FINE to fall asleep to this one. It's sometimes called "lazy qigong" because you don't have to interact with this CD, just listen till you fall asleep.

Remember: the body heals best when relaxed.

Chi Healing Meditation (Lachi) CD (60 min) - I did this one on days when I only used the DVD

2 times (once or twice a week)

In terms of time spent per session, my advice is to aim for minimum time slots of 40 minutes whenever you can, to ensure the opportunity for deeper practice. When you can, it's great do 80 or more minutes at a time - it really intensifies the experience. If you work, I would recommend trying this on weekends when possible.

Afterthoughts:

This bears repeating: Please do not get into negative territory by chastising yourself by not having the perfect form exhibited on the DVDs. Be pleased that you find yourself where you are, doing what you are doing. Visualize improvement, without expecting it. Allow yourself to be pleasantly surprised.

Short practice is great to use when out and about. I do subtle Iachi practice (see brown CD) when waiting on line at the market, or in an office, etc. Also, I use the word "Haola", meaning "All is well" as a silent mantra I repeat to myself when walking. Try to keep your relationship to the energy field open, alive, and sustained as often as possible. When I hear of a tragedy on the news, I often meditate, sending healing energy thoughts to all involved.

Some would call this prayer.

7
Sound Healing

"For me singing sad songs often has a way of healing a situation. It gets the hurt out into the open, into the light, out of the darkness."

- *Reba McEntire*

One of the most frequent requests/concerns I receive from those working with the Inner Vibrational Sound Healing CD is about correctly making the sounds. I know from my own experience, and now from working with so many challenged by the PD condition, that there is often an almost paralyzing desire for perfection in performance. For many, this seems to generate an all-or-nothing approach. Anxiety over perfection often prevents action. I don't find this attitude at all supportive of healing.

The good news is that intention is of utmost importance and strongly overpowers any sincere "mistakes" that may be made as one begins to learn the process. When I began practicing Sound Healing, I had no phonetic pronunciation charts available; I just struggled along and did my best to mimic the sounds I heard on the CD. Still a great healing occurred.

Now, however, this information is available, and I am about to share it here as well. I do this to hopefully help alleviate anxiety over perfection, not to contribute to the stress factor. So at the end of this chapter, please find a pronunciation guide. This is simply a tool. My hope is that it will help you enjoy the practice, which is a very powerful one.

This chart accompanies the SINGLE ($15.00) Inner Vibrational Sound Healing CD available from the Chi Center. This is the only CD I know of that includes the sound for the brain. I made the sound every day and visualized my brain as though strung with holiday lights of all colors, blinking and interacting with each other.

PRONUNCIATION CHART (Except for the brain, all organs have 3 sounds, representing the physical, emotional and spiritual aspects.)

BRAIN SOUND: Sun-gee

HEART:

  Physical: Sheen;

  Emotional: She-ong;

  Spiritual: Sheen-g

KIDNEY:

  Physical: Eh;

  Emotional: Ee-you;

  Spiritual: Y-ing

DIGESTION:

  Physical: Gong;

  Emotional: Foo;

  Spiritual: Dz-awng

LIVER:

Physical: Tu;

Emotional: J-eu;

Spiritual: Ling (rhymes with 'sing')

LUNGS:

First: Sawng;

Second: Si-Ssss;

Third: Sonngg

COLORS and ELEMENTS:

HEART: red or pink (fire)

KIDNEY: dark blue or black (water)

DIGESTIVE SYSTEM: gold (earth)

LIVER: green (wood)

LUNGS: white or silver (metallic)

To find the single CD I used, go to

www.chicenter.com

Also available on that site is a 2-CD sound healing set, it is NOT the one I used and does NOT include the sound for the brain. It does, however, come with a lovely booklet and an elegant sound guide chart.

Afterthoughts:

The more I learn about healing, the more I believe in the significance of vibration. At the time I sought AIT, Auditory Integration Training, and then Sensory Integration Training for my autistic son, I wasn't interested in the means, just the outcome. And the outcome was a much enhanced life quality for Justin.

His speech and walk became fluid, his language use exploded from extremely laconic to poetic. At sixteen, he began playing with words the way a young child does. It was fascinating watching him go through language development at fast forward. Right after both treatments, while he was rewiring, I now perceive that a "chi-reaction" type event occurred. There were a few huge behavioral/ emotional meltdowns as his circuits were adjusting. Then he settled into his higher level of functioning.

So it seems to me that there are many ways to approach sound healing. Several of these are presented by Judith Kahleani Lynne and Suzanne Jonas. (See Appendix.)

Also, in his book, *Wisdom Healing (Zhineng) Qigong: Activate and Embody Wisdom and Energy For Health, Healing, And Happiness*, Mingtong Gu cites several medical studies in the "Scientific Insight" sections on pp. 152 and 153.

For more about Auditory Integration Training, "The Sound of a Miracle" by Annabelle Stelhi is an account by a mother of her daughter's emergence from autism via the AIT method.

8
Permission to Heal

"It's a sad day when you learn that it's not accident or time or fortune, but yourself that keeps things from you."

- Lillian Hellman

I am contacted regularly by a number of people with Parkinson's and some of them perplex me. They want to know if I really practiced for several hours a day because they don't have the time for that. It seems to me that all serious chronic conditions are screaming at us to pay attention and to devote positive time and energy to making ourselves well NOW before any further deterioration occurs. The "pay now or pay later" adage applies so well here. That job that seems so important can and will be done by someone else at some point down the road anyway. I know, having been forced by Parkinson's to retire from teaching. The good news was, within a year of retirement I had found qigong and begun recovery.

I think the "no time" issue may be an uncon-
scious cover-up of something bigger: the
question, "Do I deserve to take the time to
work on healing myself? What about my
family, friends, co-workers, obligations,
finances?" What about them if the Parkinson's
continues to progress?

Why not try a time-out for jump-starting
recovery? How about a good three months?
Three months of several daily hours of qigong
to attempt to rewire a lifetime of neurological
overload does not seem unreasonable. Had the
diagnosis been brain cancer, and several months
needed for treatment and recovery, most would
not hesitate to find the time then. Or had
dialysis been necessary, time would have been
taken from work.

I remember the difficulty I had in signing up for
my initial introductory qigong weekend
workshop. I had already been spending
retirement funds on hiring someone to do the
things around the house I could no longer do,
like carrying boxes up and down stairs because
my balance was off. My budget was tight. But

I decided, with coaxing from a friend, that just maybe this could help, and I was desperate for relief from pain and fatigue. It was during that first Wisdom Healing Qigong weekend that I decided to sign up for the China retreat to take place in three months' time. I didn't know that in the interim I would experience powerful healing and recover from much of the Parkinson's condition before I ever went to China.

Truly, I believe that both decisions: to attend the workshop and to go to Guelin, China, were healing in themselves, prior to participating in the actual events. It was a huge deal for me to step up to the plate for myself. To realize that all the loved ones and responsibilities I was concerned about would be better served when I began to better serve myself!

So I do understand the initial hesitation to take the necessary measures to support one's own healing. My mission is to encourage the undecided. If you're even contemplating my suggestion, you are listening to an inner voice that would serve you well in being further cultivated. "Just Say Yes." Now is the time for you to care for yourself, your primary obligation on this planet.

Afterthoughts:

It may seem daunting to attempt three hours of practice per day. I have heard from someone who is practicing about one hour a day and getting very good results. Again, the idea is to have a dedicated daily practice. For me, it means as much as eating or sleeping.

9
A Word About Medications

"For me, energy became my medicine."

- Bianca Mollé

I realize that one difference between myself and some other PWP's brave enough to go public is that I had a history of medication. This makes my story of particular interest to the many, like myself, who were prescribed palliative drugs soon after their diagnosis. It would be irresponsible of me not to address this issue, as I want no one out there to hear part of my story and then throw away their pills.

It just doesn't work like that, and my conscience will not allow me to share my experience without the proper caveats. Again, I must state that I am not a medical professional and only share anecdotal experience.

I was on Sinemet 25/00 for about a year, with a

brief digression when attempting no meds, and then trying Mirapex. There was a hasty return to Sinemet, and within a few months Requip XL was added, one time daily. Still, my condition was worsening.

I consulted with the neurologist about worsening pain and was told, once again, that there is no pain with Parkinson's. That was in April, 2009. That June, I began practicing qigong, and each time felt a little more opening, a bit less stiffness, and less fatigue. Sometimes tremor and pain seemed intensified (often part of the healing process), but I am grateful that my thinking was already so positive that I never considered this a signal to increase meds. It was evident to me that, in general, I was on the mend.

The first time I forgot to take the scheduled dose of Sinemet, I panicked. The next time my reaction was different. I was already learning to listen to my body, and regarded the "forgetting" as a message that maybe I didn't need to take meds as often. But how does one wean oneself from meds that affect the brain? The words "slowly" and "carefully" came to mind. I wanted assistance, but didn't know where to find it.

I quickly dismissed asking any of the neurologists I was seeing. They just weren't yet comfortable with a patient interested in self-empowerment, nor did I think they were ready for the concept that one could heal from PD. I tried a few stealthy calls to pharmacists, who quickly deduced my plans and refused the information. I'm sure they thought they were acting in my best interest.

I was planning to attend the Healing Intensive Retreat in China, and wanted to be free of medications prior to my trip, so that I could work with any remaining symptoms in their full-blown glory. In subsequent medical records, the neurologist describes what I did as "titrating" (myself) off Sinemet. I'm not a chemist and not certain that what I did fits the layman's definition of "titration" and feel I must say this so as not to mislead anyone.

I visited the neurologist prior to my trip to show off my reduced symptoms and to ask how to come off the Requip XL. He was impressed with how I was faring off the Sinemet, even though my tremor was in full force, partly, I'm sure, in reaction to my own insecurity in facing this medical authority. He did give me the information I requested about Requip, but informed me that when one reduces or comes off one medication, the other drug would need to be increased. I told him I thought not, and prepared for my trip.

About a year or so into my recovery I began reading "Almost Icarus" by Janice Walton-Hadlock. I was horror-struck with the idea that someone could hear my story and be irresponsibly inspired to play with their medication, perhaps with life-threatening results. For a time, I wanted to reverse the clock and keep my story, or at least the meds part of it, a secret.

But the cat was already out of the bag, and I had to assume for a reason. Perhaps the reason is to give hope to the many who find themselves currently in situations similar to my own recovery starting point. Although I cannot and do not give out medical advice, I can here explain my situation, what it felt like to me, and what I have learned after the fact:

As one continues with a daily POSITIVE

practice (enjoying the practice itself, not setting up expectations for results or demanding self-perfection, i.e., RELAXING), energy starts to flow and opens blockages. At times this feels wonderful: more energy, less pain, stiffness and fatigue. At other times one can experience more pain, fatigue, and tremor. This does not necessarily mean the condition is worsening and more drugs are necessary. Often this is when major healing occurs.

And here's another piece of confusing information. One should not hurry to reduce medications or have a pre-planned "titration schedule." The message my body gave me was in the forgetting to take scheduled doses. Someone else's bodily message may be different. At the same time, as the practice continues and real healing occurs, not as much medication may be necessary, and overmedication may feel like undermedication (i.e., overmedication may result in increased symptoms). What a lot to swallow (pardon the pun).

So what to do? I have been told that compounding pharmacists may be of assistance, yet they seem hard to come by, and not all may be willing to take on such a challenge. A number of people have found websites with different suggestions for various schedules of medication reduction. And it is my thought that one simply does not go along with a reduction schedule if the body isn't quite there yet.

It is my hope that as we increase in number there will be more published information, and more professionals at the ready to assist. There are a number of people out there reversing symptoms and reducing meds. It is only a matter of time till there are more healing stories.

Is working on recovery worth facing this challenge? I can only answer from my personal vantage point that when I began the practice, I was looking for some relief and a way to avoid increasing meds, and perhaps, if I were lucky, even more. Full recovery happened, and in the process I had to deal with the medications, and did so successfully. I don't believe myself to be the only one. Recovery isn't easy, but it's better than the alternative.

I am pleased to learn that Dr. Robert Rogers of www.parkinsonsrecovery.com (robert@parkinsonsrecovery.com) offers consultations around managing Parkinson's drugs while recovering.

Disclaimer: This was written for informational purposes only. It is not suggested medical advice for any individual. Content should not be considered medical advice. The writer is not a medical professional.

10

WHEN? The Slower You Go, the Faster You Heal!

"Let go of your attachment to outcome . . . Endeavors accomplished quickly and easily rarely endure."

- Taro Gold

I attended a daylong workshop on Insight Meditation on Saturday, led by the wise and witty Howard Cohn at the beautiful Spirit Rock facility here in Marin County. The concepts of "wanting" and "avoiding" were themes presented. Let's look at how that applies to the health situation.

We all "want" good health, and thus "want to avoid" the onset or worsening of the symptoms that Parkinson's or any chronic health challenge presents. It is healthy to want for ourselves that which is wholesome. What becomes unwholesome and self-defeating is running the clock on our desires.

Every day I hear from people all over the planet, in various stages of PD, and some in stages of recovery. Almost without exception, they want to know when a certain symptom began to abate or totally disappear for me. Fortunately, I didn't note dates for these events, but I did celebrate each and every small improvement.

However, even if I had noted dates, I would find it irresponsible to share them. I remind everyone that each individual heals differently, just as the condition manifests differently in each person. Furthermore, it is totally counterproductive to watch the clock, moving a step away from healing, as I see it.

As I was reminded by Howard Cohn on Saturday, we need to be "in the moment" in order to connect with our healing sources and places. This is an essential component of meditation, and I know that the meditative mind has been essential to my healing. Simple, yes. Easy, far from it. But that is the challenge that healing from chronic conditions presents, and that I now highlight for you.

Use the future not for increased anxiety over timelines, but to visualize yourself with increased health and expressing the gratitude that follows. That is the recommended way to dwell in the future.

I understand how strong the desire is to be rid of the symptoms, especially tremors, which for many are the trademark and constant reminder of the Parkinson's condition. I admit, I felt that way at times, too. It was difficult for me to not constantly hold my hands out before me, to see if there was tremor, and if so, how did it measure up to the last time I looked - more or less intense? When I spoke to Mingtong about this, he cautioned me against it.

So I then exerted the effort to control myself, and was successful a good deal, though not all, of the time. I did, however, begin to understand that healing is a mysterious process. Remember, the chi energy itself may manifest as vibration, especially in the hands. So, how can you be certain to distinguish that which is tremor from that which is healing energy? Then why not view this movement, especially if it occurs during practice, as a part of the healing? That's what I did, and I don't regret the outcome.

So, my chi chums, haste makes waste, and perhaps even exacerbates illness at times. Savor your practice and your progress. Celebrate that you even navigated to this page as part of your healing process. Remember that when you were learning to walk, sometimes you fell: but it was all part of the learning-to-walk process.

So don't beat yourself up if you've been watching the clock, just start right now practicing to turn away from it. And if a tremor or some other symptom seems more noticeable today than it was yesterday, don't discount that it may be part of your healing process.

When you are totally involved in the present moment, relaxed and grateful to be alive and for the many blessings in your life, this is when your body opens up to healing. I believe it was my qigong teacher, Mingtong Gu, who said: "The slower you go, the faster you heal." Ironic, counter-intuitive, but true. When I first heard this statement, I thought it referred only to the physical movements of the qigong practice. Now I understand how it applies to so much more. Calendars are helpful for keeping appointments and for celebrating events. Not for trying to force a healing outcome.

Afterthoughts:

As I now deal with sporadic leg pain issues, and therefore sometimes limit my activity level, I remind myself of the conversation I had with my inner self, the body-mind-spirit convention I held one evening shortly after my Parkinson's diagnosis. I asked the disease to be my teacher, said that I was ready to learn. I must remember that for me it is helpful to view all challenges in this way. It is the path away from the negative spiral.

11
And the Winning Number is . . .

"Ever since happiness heard your name, it has been running through the streets to find you."

– Hafiz of Persia

Anyone who has sat in one of my writing classes knows that I have always emphasized audience awareness. Many papers were returned with comments like "tone too informal for your audience" or "need to develop awareness of who will read this before you write." Yet, here I sit, not really knowing my audience personally, and my musings are of such a personal nature. This was a concern because I wanted to please you with what I offered.

Then came the conundrum: I believe you want the truth of my experience, and what if you don't like that? I know that the truth of my experience, as I perceive it, must be why you are currently reading this book. Many of you may be diagnosed with Parkinson's Disease or some other condition that finds little solace in the resources of Western medicine. You've decided to explore alternative methods. That's where I found myself after over a year on two different Parkinson's medications, and a condition that was worsening.

I didn't want to increase the medications and was looking for another way to find relief from the pain, stiffness, fatigue, shaking, lack of balance, swallowing issues . . . the list goes on. This description does not necessarily portray a happy camper. Yet, I was not simply the sum total of every adjective previously portrayed. That is, I was not the condition, but so much more, and I clung closely to that comforting belief. It allowed for happiness.

Then I began practicing Zhineng Qigong and immediately gained some relief, which grew incrementally, until fifteen months later (after a year of no Parkinson's drugs), I was pronounced symptom-free of PD by the neuro-logist.

How could this be? This disease is supposed to

be incurable, irreversible, and progressive. And I am a mere mortal, usually well-intentioned, but far from saintly or perfect - my family, friends, and students would be first to agree. So how did this amazing healing occur?

I must admit, I felt a bit like Harry Potter, bumbling about Hogwarts, being celebrated for something and not knowing the how or why of it, and sometimes embarrassed and/or confused by the praise and attention. Nevertheless, I openly share this event, and often rejoice in it.

Keyword: Rejoice!! My message is to celebrate every little improvement, to self-reward for even making the decision to learn about qigong. That was what I did. When my shoulders became less stiff and less painful, I put on a cd and danced around the house till I wore myself out. I didn't wait for every symptom to disappear before I began enjoying my recovery.

In fact, I have become such a party animal that I celebrate every April 29th, as that was the date in 2008 that I received my diagnosis. It seems to me that there could be a real connection between improved happiness and upgraded health.

Then I read a book that confirmed what I knew intuitively about the power of joy, plus explained so much more. Now I return to my original audience dilemma. I am finding the answers to my questions about healing in the areas often termed as "soft science." I have always been a practical person - pretty open, but too busy dealing with the here and now of the material world to spend time wondering about the universe and how it operates. But that is where my current situation has brought me.

As I coach clients with Parkinson's Disease, I want to give them more than a "to-do" list to follow. Yes, the best way to get where I am (for some, there are many ways to restore health) is to follow closely what I did, but what about the "how" of it? If I could somehow explain that, would it perhaps bring an added advantage? So that was the question I posed to myself, and I found an answer that works for me in the book *Power VS Force* by David R. Hawkins, M.D., Ph.D.

Hawkins, who co-authored a book on orthomolecular psychiatry with Linus Pauling, assigns every emotion a vibrational level. The higher the frequency, the better we feel, and vice-versa. Shame resonates at 20, guilt 30, fear 100, love 500. Both healing and joy resonate at the same frequency: 540. So my intuitive hit about celebrating during the healing process was right on.

If I haven't lost you yet, you may be wondering how these emotions came to be calibrated. Here I invite you to travel a bit further into "woo-woo" territory with me. Muscle testing was used. It is explained in the book, or you can research it online.

Basically, this method believes that inner self knows the answers and that the body reflects these truths. It's all about vibration, and how every living thing vibrates in some way. We all want to raise our vibrational levels to feel better, and in so doing we can often raise the vibrations of those around us.

I'm still basically a bonehead when it comes to the healing arts and the world of energy. But that's what restored my health and vitality, and I will work tirelessly to figure it out and explain it because I want others to be able to experience the happiness, health, and second chance at life that I currently enjoy.

Perhaps the one and only thing we can control is our emotions. The power of positive thinking is not a new idea. Its practical application and the scope of its potential is something to be explored. Just think about all the songs and maxims that invite us to do just that. From "Whistle a Happy Tune" to "Raindrops on Roses and Whiskers on Kittens" to "Let a Smile Be Your Umbrella" to "Don't Worry Be Happy".

And those two Normans, Cousins and Vincent Peale, brought us the same ideas sans the music. The physiology of smiling, even a forced smile, is considered healthier than the opposite. We can sometimes "happy" our way to health, the challenge is being willing to work at the consciousness and self-awareness it takes to begin. Five-hundred forty is just around the corner. Meet me there.

Afterthoughts:

Since this piece was written I have become acquainted with a book called "The Happiness Advantage" by Shawn Achor. Mr. Achor,

Harvard researcher and lecturer, espouses the idea that "happiness fuels success" instead of vice-versa. If success means recovering from a disease, I would suggest one start with being happy that the possibility exists, that you have seen proof of it in recovery stories, and that you are now working on it yourself. This is something to celebrate. Reboot your brain, and rejoice in the process!

12
The Lion Sleeps Tonight

"You must never be fearful about what you are doing when it is right."

- Rosa Parks

In case I seem brimming with gratitude, I have learned to savor all that is going right in my life, and truly believe vibrational levels are raised and healing intensified by this practice. That being said, one more giant burst of gratitude erupts for Dr. Robert Rodgers for The Parkinson's Recovery Summit in Cincinnati in June, 2012.

An amazing space of compassion and healing was created. I met so many wonderful people and felt honored to present my workshop, "One Stop Shopping for Healing," to an audience of so many motivated seekers. The conference held numerous highlights. One that has remained for me is a lovely meditation Robert led one evening.

We were reminded that the Parkinson's mind is accustomed to running with adrenalin, keeping the body in constant "fight or flight" mode, as though being chased by a lion 24/7. Robert encouraged us to visualize a switch where we could revert back to dopamine when not in crisis. This thought coincided with my recent stage of recovery.

Yes, the physical symptoms of Parkinson's left some time ago, and I have been gradually observing my own recovery in the mental/ emotional areas now. I think sharing that may be of some value. So I'd like to take you through some recent events (challenges) and share how differently they were experienced via recovery, with daily meditative and physical qigong.

Picture a retired schoolteacher and grandmother who a few years earlier thought her life was, at least in some ways, over, now preparing to travel cross-country to present a workshop. Let's go back even one step further, to being invited to present the workshop. My first thought was: "No way!" Then I remembered how alive I feel every time I challenge my own comfort zone. I also knew I had a message of hope to share, and didn't want my own selfish lack of confidence to prevent me from helping others. So I accepted and immediately felt it was the right decision by the relief I experienced from saying "Yes."

Cut to the baggage carousel at the Greater Cincinnati Airport. In previous travels, I can recall that sense of doom that my suitcase wouldn't appear (based somewhat on prior experience). This time I noticed how relaxed I was, even as I positioned myself in the crowd of passengers. I no longer had to claim that certain spot exactly where the bags emerge. If my luggage were there, it would turn the corner with everyone else's. If not, it would either appear with the next flight, or restitution would be made by the airline - perhaps inconvenient, but not a lion at my back by any means!

Then, when it was time to present my workshop, more challenges arose. The elevator bank leading down to the conference center wasn't operating, and when I maneuvered with all my materials to the stairwell, the door was locked. Finally, someone came to repair the elevator, and I entered the room at 8 am, the exact time my workshop was scheduled to begin, along with the crowd that was my audience. New process: I didn't feel any anger or disappointment with myself. I wasn't afraid that my presentation would fail. These inconveniences were beyond my control.

My audience understood, and a number of people volunteered to help with setting up and handing out materials. It was like being back in my middle school classroom, assisted by student aides. Then the CD player I had lugged all the way from SF refused to work - so I sang instead. Once again, lion averted. (At least for me, perhaps not for those who had to hear me sing!)

One final example occurred just the other day. I was negotiating a turn onto my street when a car that should have observed a stop sign didn't. The driver managed to stop within a few feet of me - I could even see the remorseful expression on his face. What amazed me was that I experienced some anxiety/fear/excitement in the moment, but only in the moment. Within a few seconds I felt calm and normal again. The lion barely yawned.

In my bedroom, on the wall that faces my bed, is a print of Rousseau's "The Sleeping Gypsy." The gypsy is peacefully asleep in beautiful rainbow-colored garb, with the lion awake, wide-eyed, beside the sleeping form. The relationship of the two, or "story" is left to the observer. What is your lion doing tonight?

Afterthoughts:

Up till now my "going public" was something that just organically happened, beyond my control. I was speaking at a qigong weekend about my recovery from Parkinson's Disease several years ago, and unbeknownst to me, Lilou Mace and her "Juicy Living Tour" film crew were in the audience. The next thing I knew, my interview was on YouTube.

That debut was quickly followed by an invitation from Dr. Robert Rodgers to be interviewed on his internet radio broadcast. At that point Robert told me I'd need a website and blog, and he was correct. Emails began pouring in, and it was necessary to find a comprehensive way to address some questions and issues.

I never thought of myself as being involved in a controversy: hard medical science vs. woo-woo. Nor had I expected to be viewed by some as a fraud or "snake oil" salesman. I was simply getting out a message that I thought at least some would find helpful, and offering further assistance if sought. And that experience has, to a great extent, been positive.

Now I feel compelled to go beyond that. To put in bold print the thoughts and experiences that I believe could be helpful to others. Sometimes I feel anxiety knocking at the back door. At least now it's using the back door, and at least now I know I don't have to open it. My interest is no longer in pleasing everyone, and I do not fear any negativity that may come my way. I am confident in my intention and seek continued guidance in meditation. Haola.

13

Pain and Parkinson's Disease

"Do you not see how necessary a world of pains and troubles is to school an intelligence and make it a soul?"

- John Keats

One of the daily miracles I celebrate since healing from Parkinson's Disease is waking up pain-free every day. Haola! Not only that, but in the evening I can sleep on my side again, either side. I am no longer paralyzed by painfully stiff shoulder blades. This morning I remembered another cause for gratitude: doing fine motor work without stiffness, clumsiness, or pain. Today is my grandson, Alex's, fourth birthday. I was able to wrap his presents neatly and precisely, using tape and wrapping paper. For many years, long prior to my diagnosis, I had switched over to using gift bags - the only way any gift from me could appear presentable - just ask my friends. My godchild's mom used to secretly re-wrap my gifts before giving them to her daughter!

The reason the topic of pain comes up is that last week I was reminded of what it feels like to be told there is no pain with Parkinson's Disease. Tuesday was my first neurology visit in two years. The last time I had been seen and declared "symptom free" I was told to return in one year if there were issues, or in two years if I remained symptom-free. So I made my return visit and was dismissed from the neurology department: a wonderful event!

Since the neurologist I had seen two years prior had moved to a different office, I was seen by someone new. Her thorough examination was the one that dismissed me. She was very interested in my case and in reviewing my diagnosis. I went over my original long list of presenting symptoms, and we were in agreement with all, except that she, like her previous colleague, insisted that there was no pain with PD. Back in the spring of 2009, when I was seen by her predecessor, I had complained of pain, fatigue, and having arms and legs that felt heavy, like they were weighted down with sandbags. He insisted that there was no pain with Parkinson's, but that often depression occurred, which could include sensations of physical pain. So I was referred by him to the psychiatrist.

How did I feel about all this? Like it was adding insult to injury. However, my life was becoming so compromised that I told myself to jump through any hoop if it would point in the direction of possible relief. So in June of 2009 I was seen by a psychiatrist. I told him I didn't think I was depressed, because depressed people don't want to do much of anything. I, on the other hand, wanted to do everything, and was becoming increasingly frustrated that I couldn't. He listened, asked questions, administered what I believe was Beck's Depression Inventory. His conclusion was that I was not depressed, but experiencing pain, fatigue, and difficulty with movement.

On the one hand, I was validated. On the other hand, I was almost disappointed. If it had been depression, as predicted, then maybe a pill could have helped. My shrinking life was continuing to contract, along with my muscles. Fortunately for me, it was two days later that I was first introduced to Wisdom Healing Qigong and began to experience immediately both hope and relief.

That was the start of my return to health and freedom from PD. Since then, in recent years, I have spoken to many groups about my healing. I have established a practice as a wellness coach and consultant, and have a client and reader base composed of people with Parkinson's and/or their families or caregivers, and of people with other chronic conditions. Not all complain of pain, but many do.

After a recent speaking engagement, I was approached by a gentleman who thanked me for addressing the pain that can accompany this condition. He, too, had been quoted the party line of "no pain with PD." So after I returned from my neurology visit the other day, I decided to do a little research around pain and Parkinson's.

The Cleveland Clinic addresses pain and Parkinson's with Central Pain Syndrome, defined as: "... a neurological condition caused by damage to or dysfunction of the central nervous system which includes the brain, brainstem, and spinal cord. This syndrome can be caused by stroke, MS, tumors, epilepsy, brain or spinal cord trauma or Parkinson's Disease . . ."

The article goes on to describe the possible locations, varieties, intensities, and durations of pain - and it's not pretty. NIDS, The National Institute of Nervous Disorders and Stroke, uses the exact same definition for Central Pain Syndrome, including Parkinson's in the list of painful contributing conditions.

I felt like I opened up the closet and uncovered the Bogeyman whom I was told didn't exist: Central Pain Syndrome. So there you have it. Yes, Virginia, there can be pain with Parkinson's Disease, and I hope those who have been told otherwise find this information helpful. Feeling pain is painful enough. It may lessen the anxiety to learn it isn't necessarily imagined.

Afterthoughts:

I realize that in recounting my experience with Western medicine in the treatment of

Parkinson's disease, there is no positive support mentioned. That was the truth of my experience. It doesn't mean that there aren't a growing number of MD's who see the benefit of combining Western medicine with Traditional Chinese medicine, herbs and homeopathy. Plus there are popular "celebrity" physicians like Deepak Chopra and Mehmet Oz, who are open to energetic and other types of healing. Amit Goswami, Ph.D., has written the book *Quantum Doctor*, hoping to popularize the idea of all fields of healing working together cooperatively. Integral medicine is a term with quickly widening usage.

14

Parkinson's on the Job: To Tell or Not to Tell?

"If you obsess over whether or not you are making the right decision, you are basically assuming that the universe will reward you for one thing and punish you for another."

- Deepak Chopra

How does one handle the situation when the Parkinson's symptoms become visible/diagnosed? I was ignorant of the fact that several colleagues had noticed "something was going on" long prior to my disclosure of this personal information. Often PWPs, Persons with Parkinson's, are at or near the summit of their careers or lifetime roles when the condition manifests. In some ways I was at the top of my teaching game after twenty-five years on the job, yet at times I felt the rug slipping out from under me. After a few years of floundering around, including a futile attempt to alleviate growing distractability/disorganization with Ritalin, I discovered PD was the responsible culprit. I had already submitted my retirement papers several months prior to this diagnosis, knowing that I wasn't well enough to carry on, but not knowing why.

So in April of 2008 I was given the drug Sinemet 25/100 as part of a diagnostic tool. If the symptoms began to abate with the use of the drug, Parkinson's would be confirmed. There was a caveat: among possible side effects were hallucinations. Up to this point, I had no intention of sharing my health situation with any of my colleagues till after my retirement.

Now there was a dilemma. I was still on duty in the middle-school classroom for two more months. What if I tripped out in class? Although I thought the odds of this eventuality were slim, I felt I owed it to my students to fully disclose the situation to my principal so that he could be prepared to handle the situation, should it arise.

Fortunately for me, I was able to complete my final months in the classroom with ease. No harm no foul. In some ways, I was very lucky. On the other hand, had I not allowed myself to go so long without diagnosis and treatment, perhaps I'd still be in the eighth-grade classroom today. I know a piece of my heart will always remain there, which, along with making up financially for early retirement, is why I love to substitute teach.

I realize that retiring early is nowhere near as difficult as is facing the limitations of Parkinson's when one is mid-career. More and more I hear from people younger than myself who are in this quandary. With some exceptions, they are keeping it to themselves. I get it. Completely. They don't want to be identified for so many good reasons - besides not wanting pity. There is career ladder and job security to consider. In this day and age, many are also currently without any or adequate health insurance and fear the dire consequences of such a health revelation.

Ironically, this creates extreme added pressure which can aggravate symptoms. There are laws to protect, support, and defend those with disabilities, but in order to use them, one must first decide "come out" and deal with reactions, which can be very difficult. Also, PWPs can be quite stubborn. I am the parent of an autistic child and spent part of my earlier years teaching in the Special Education classroom. I knew what limitations looked like.

Yet, I never considered myself disabled. Instead, I just got angry with myself for the difficulties experienced. (So glad I finally learned about the healing power of self-love!)

There is no conclusion at this point. Each situation is unique to each individual. I have heard stories of people in other cultures being lovingly supported in their work by their families and communities, so that Parkinson's was never really an issue. Perhaps the best we can do is right here, right now, begin a virtual support system for ourselves, a place to share the on-the-job issues faced by challenged bodies with passionate spirits. I suspect this will be an ongoing and/or revisited topic. As Labor Day approaches, let's be grateful for the jobs and skills we have and continue to lovingly care for ourselves so that we may carry on in the best possible fashion. For me, right now, that means it's time to meditate.

Afterthoughts:

The lead-in quote I selected for this chapter strongly resonated for me with how I used to make decisions, always fearing some unknown wrath could be part of the outcome. The equanimity I have gained since my healing shows me that a mindful and fearless decision can never be all wrong. Again, it comes to self-trust, which is not really possible without self-love. Also, although I thought my condition was a "secret," when I spilled the beans I found out that a few astute people (perhaps more) had figured out that something was happening with my health. So maybe the decision of "telling or not telling" was not completely in my control. My body was already betraying me. Each individual must make the personal decision of "if" and "when" to tell. I'm just presenting my own personal experience around the issue to provide fodder for thought.

15
The Feeling Aspect of Healing

"One's suffering disappears when one lets oneself go, when one yields-even to sadness."

- Antoine de St. Exupéry

Prior to my own healing experience via the mind-body connection, the suggestion of a relationship between emotions and healing would have probably been lost on me. Now that I've learned how to process such a concept, I would like to help explain it to those who may be at a similar starting point to my own when I began three years ago. It seems, from recent feedback, that sharing this process can help others on their road to recovery. Also, I wish to make it clear that I believe oftentimes, as it was my in own case, Parkinson's can arise from combination of causes, a "Perfect Storm" of heredity, environmental toxins, emotional stress, weakened immune systems, and many more factors can play a role in contributing to this condition. Each person's etiology is unique to itself.

Parkinson's is a very real experience. Stress can be a contributor. It is this factor that I examine here. Not the original stress of negative emotions at the time they are experienced, but the further hardship caused by not immediately working through these feelings.

So how can one inadvertently contribute to his/her own decline in health? By refusing to allow the self to experience the feelings at the time they occur. "Powering through" can be a survival tool - until it is so overused and abused that the integrated self becomes contracted in mind, body, and spirit.

Opening to healing means processing the feeling. Keyword: Process. Move it in and out; don't allow it to sit and stagnate. I used to wonder how I could ever accomplish this without a major meltdown. I exercised tremendous self-control, afraid to unleash the seismic waves of emotion that ran beneath. As my recovery continued and my practice evolved, I found much greater equanimity.

I mentioned in a recent blog about almost having a vehicular collision. Yes, I felt a healthy amount of fear, and it came and went very quickly. This was such a different experience for me that I noted it.

Another example from much earlier on in my recovery occurred in the summer of 2009, almost immediately following my initial introduction to qigong. I couldn't understand what was happening in my body. The pain and stiffness of Parkinson's, along with many of the other symptoms, had begun to recede. Yet a frequent wet cough had developed. At first I thought it could be a summer cold or the flu.

However, that didn't quite compute, as I didn't feel sick at all. As a matter of fact, I felt increasingly better each day. The cough lasted for five or six weeks, during which time I learned that in Chinese medicine the lungs are the organs that house grief. I had been practicing both physical qigong and sound healing daily. When my emotional floodgates were opened, grief was the first emotion to come charging through. As grief was transformed into joy, the vibrational spiral began its upward trajectory. The happiness/

fulfillment factor is exponential. The initial transformation promotes further fulfillment, and so on. One of the many reasons I continue to practice daily. HAOLA!

Afterthoughts:

I remember attending a meditation class at Spirit Rock Meditation Center just prior to discovering qigong. For once, I seemed to be able to mentally get beyond my itchy nose and grocery list. I was at calm and at peace. Yet tears began to stream down my face. As we finished the meditation, Anna Douglas, our teacher, mentioned that often tears come as a release. Perhaps they were in a decades-long cue, waiting for me to allow them to make their gentle journey.

16
Navigating Relationships

"Many times the best way to fight is not to fight at all."

- Taro Gold

I am not an expert in healing from Parkinson's Disease. I am only an expert in my own healing from Parkinson's Disease. Now I attempt to reflect on it and see if others can find this information useful. So please, read all with a critical eye, and bring a shoehorn along to see if it's the right fit for you.

As I continue to work with others recovering from PD, I am beginning to notice patterns emerge. As the inner and outer selves begin to unify, responses to situations start to change. Awakening intensifies and vitality increases. The zombie-like straight jacket loosens both physically and emotionally. Good? Yes. Easy? No!

In recovery, myself and those I work with become more aware of our own needs and desires. This is part of the authentic self that begins to break through. Sometimes giving oneself more of "yes" can mean giving someone else a little more "no." It's not surprising that this is not always well-received by those around us.

Many of us have spent a lifetime people-pleasing, so we are unaccustomed to consider-ing ourselves, and unprepared for the surprised response such behavior can elicit from others. Especially initially, this doesn't always feel good. Yet, it does feel better than self-denial, and builds positively from there. More good news follows.

I find myself gradually becoming more comfortable in standing up for myself. The equanimity brought about by meditation allows me to accept the difficulty others may have with the "new me" as part of the healing process - my own, and perhaps theirs as well. I must mention here that I find it possible, and most preferable, to support myself without creating conflict with others. The way to do this is to state the situation, as perceived by me, objectively.

In the past, "defending" myself was accompanied by emotional turmoil that often resulted in physical shaking. Now, I am able to calmly express myself, often with a smile. The payoff is that this does not feel at all phony, and I feel better afterwards. I am no longer worried about reprisals. If I am true to myself, and kind to others, all is well.

There is a concurrent way to view this situation, and it has to do with vibrational level. See essay titled "And the Winning Number is 540." Basically, the higher the vibration, the better we feel: in mind, body, and spirit. Hence we see the relationship between joy and healing. Dopamine, anyone?

So, being the self-appointed Monday-morning quarterback for healing from PD, here's my take-away: As vibrational level changes, it brings some relationships closer to us, and distances us from others. As with physical healing, this is a gradual process. The caveat here is not to put the cart before the horse and attempt to control the situation by pushing relationship buttons. Focus on healing the self, and sit back and notice what happens. There is no need to add chaos or drama to an already challenging situation. Not easy, I know. Especially for PWP's who often focus on outcome and control. I constantly replay the Beatles "Let It Be" to assist me in noticing, not reacting.

It has taken me a while to permit myself to go public with this insight, as I know part of my own former process may have been to read something like this and then attempt to forcefully create all kinds of relational upheavals. I simply share this so you can take notice and see if the experience perhaps applies to you or explains something that is currently in process for you. There is usually no need to recalibrate the relationships in our lives. As we stay firmly moored in our practice, we may allow them to float around us, with the vibrational level, not our own self-will, determining their ebb and flow. So I'm pulling up a deck chair and waiting to receive what the tide brings in. Haola!

Afterthoughts:

I just happened to see a Dr. Oz broadcast featuring a woman who had healed from a non-Hodgkins lymphoma she had been told would kill her. She mentioned her strong desire for life, finally considering herself worthy and placing herself first, and in the process reviewing her relationships, to scan for toxicity.

17
Working Past Recovery

"God sells us all things at the price of labor."

- Leonardo da Vinci

I keep being humbled by the magnitude of this amazing concept of recovery. Three years ago at this time I was finally off all PD medications, had some pain and tremor, but had come so far from the intense pain, exhaustion, and limitations of Parkinson's that I would have been happy if the improvement had stopped there. Gratefully, it didn't. The further away I get from my time with Parkinson's Disease, the more I learn from it. It is my hope that the post-recovery challenges I mention here will help others understand what may be happening as they recover. Time at the gym is time well spent, and I have come to value, besides qigong, the Pilates Reformer machine and, once again, yoga.

Aside from my job, a writers' group, a cardmaking class and my bicycle, I had also left hiking and a regular yoga practice in the wake of my descent into disease. Hiking uphill was too painful. I felt a severe pull in my neck and shoulders. My yoga practice stopped when my wrists became too stiff for "downward facing dog", especially when I couldn't get my core to support me. I no longer found any stillness in yoga. My confused mind and trembling body were not improving. Finally, after many disappointing attempts at mind/body integration, I left the class and even stopped practicing at home. Corpse pose on the couch was the best I could muster.

(An aside here to address the question I am often asked: "Do you think the fact that you were on meds originally helped you with your qigong practice?" I would have to say: "No." I was on those same meds when I became too stiff to hike or do yoga. It seems to me it had to be the entrance of energy into my body via qigong that began the reversal of symptoms that permitted me to forget to take the meds, which was my clue that I could gradually come off them.)

I attended my first weekend workshop, purchased the DVD and CDs mentioned in my Healing Regimen, and began to practice immediately. I remember the first time I practiced LCUPCD at home, eyes closed. I began swatting at what I thought was a thick swarm of gnats flying about my head. Finally, I became so distracted I had to open my eyes. I saw nothing. It was then that I began to have some understanding of the invisible but powerful chi (energy). I never felt it in quite that way again, but the message was sent and did its job. I knew I had a powerful, though unseen, ally.

As my healing continued and the layers peeled back, leg issues began to emerge. Incorrectly, I thought these pains were part of Parkinson's and therefore, with typical Parkinson's fortitude, powered through excruciating leg pain, forcing myself into crouching positions that further wore down my knee. We were advised NOT to push through pain, to push only through discomfort. Frankly, sometimes it's still hard for me to tell the difference. Daily sound healing meditations are gradually teaching me to be aware of how my body feels.

The take-away here is that fierce determination

got me healed from Parkinson's quite rapidly. However, had I been a little gentler on myself, my leg issue would probably not have become so magnified. Do I regret this? NEVER. Did I learn from it? Yes. And I am passing that on to you. I'm not for one minute sorry about the passion with which I approached my recovery through qigong. Since I am a pioneer, why not let you be aware of this possible slight detour, so you can avoid something similar?

The good news is that after several years of limited activity, an occasional orthopedic boot, icing and elevating, my right leg is just about ready to kick some serious butt. (My own, from the sofa!) I attended my first yoga class in four years the other day. I began humbly with the easy class, and I did it!! And loved it. And as a result of over three thousand hours of qigong practice, I can now feel energy when I do yoga as well. Haola!!

I hear from a number of you who are now on your way - reversing symptoms and feeling less fatigued - and I want you to know that the end of symptoms is only the beginning of good health. As I return to a regular fitness program, I am beginning to feel my body, especially musculature, in a way I haven't for many, many years. I've learned that side-stepping is a skill that diminishes with age, so I am now including that in my routine, along with core-builders like the yoga poses of plank and bridge.

Yes, I still do qigong daily. Most days I do about two hours of qigong, including meditation, and an hour of gym (yoga or Pilates Reformer/bike/ weight training) alternately. Sounds like a bit of work. It is. But the way I see it, I was given a second chance in this body, and I will do my best to make sure all operating systems remain in good repair.

My body is a gift to be nurtured the way I nurture the gift of family and students. Parkinson's was the agent that made all this possible. The glass is always half full. Haola!

Afterthoughts:

The bulk of the above chapter was written several months ago. Now the right leg begins to thrive and the left ankle area begins to complain. My body has more lessons to teach me. Da Vinci was right!

18
The Accidental Buddhist

"If you risk nothing, then you risk everything."

- Geena Davis

So often I hear from people who want to approach healing in linear fashion. How long did it take me? Which were the first symptoms to go? These questions are understandable, yet beneath them often lies the fact that the questioner is hesitant to invest time, hopes, and perhaps a little money (for materials, classes, whatever) without a guarantee of recovery.

Most pharmaceuticals come with warning labels and caution that reactions to medications vary with individuals. I have never seen anyone harmed from practicing qigong. Even those who experience little or no physical change are glad to have found the practice and the inner peace it brings. As I was pondering this situation I happened upon a book by Pema Chodron: *108 Teachings on Cultivating Fearlessness and Compassion*. I noted how my own healing process reflected so much of this work's spiritual guidance. Hence, the conclusion that I must have been an "accidental Buddhist."

I have mentioned in an earlier post that as I began working on healing from Parkinson's with qigong, I learned of only one person who had partial success, a woman in China mentioned in Luke Chan's *101 Miracles of Natural Healing*. Because my goal was complete recovery, I was not at all attached to the few details of her story available. I didn't try to compare or mirror her results.

I treated Parkinson's as a visiting professor, and was open to whatever the lesson. I surrendered to the uncertainty of outcome. In so doing I probably spared myself much negativity and frustration. I would try qigong; there was nothing to lose. Then gains began to appear, and I had no idea if they were permanent or not. Still don't!

It's been over three years since I've had any meds, and I was declared symptom-free two years ago, and completely dismissed from neurology last month. Although I sense that my healing from this condition is permanent, there are no promises. The only thing I am guaranteed is uncertainty. I'll take it, thank you. It means I'm alive and presented with infinite possibility. It means I get to continue my relationship with uncertainty. The challenge is to do this and yet remain relaxed and positive, truly the way of the peaceful warrior. It is big work, and the battle being waged is called "not being at war with the self." Staying peaceful is the answer.

How to do this? For me, it means working with energy, beloved chi, several hours each day, and remaining aware of it throughout the day. There's a temptation, once one begins to feel a little energy and a little relief, to ease up on the discipline. That's fine if you're willing to realize that that may be as far as the healing goes. There are, of course, as stated ad nauseum, no guarantees in any case.

How many times have you heard a story about someone seeking romance who finally gave up, and Voila! A soul-mate appeared? Or how about the numerous stories of infertile couples who finally adopted or employed in-vitro fertilization, only to have child #1 closely followed by a "surprise" baby? As they relaxed and let go of outcome, wonderful manifestations appeared.

Again, no guarantee. It doesn't happen every time. The irony is that, like it or not, we are faced with uncertainty every moment of every day. However, it can be as joyful as it is frustrating. And here's the ultimate irony: When you're at war with yourself and surrender - you're victorious. Maybe even in a big way. It's a win/win situation. Haola!

Afterthoughts:

The further I come from my time with Parkinson's, the more risks I take. Yes, I challenge myself often at least partly in hopes of positive outcome, but more just to have the experience. So often the process becomes a rich reward in itself. Then if the outcome is also positive, so be it.

19
Helpful Hints

"In life we cannot do great things. We can only do small things with great love."

- Mother Theresa

It's been over three years since I began on the recovery path, and each day I learn more about my journey that may prove helpful to those facing chronic physical challenges. For several years now I've been working with students, consults, and coaching clients, and some have shared with me strategies that work for them. It has also been my good fortune to work with Dove Govrin and her Monday evening Wisdom Healing Qigong class, sponsored by Kaiser Permanente, in Terra Linda. Dove has had a focus on modifications during her decades of teaching qigong and years as a movement specialist, and her creative approach is refreshing.

I have also made modifications to my own qigong practice when a right leg, besieged with a number of non-PD related conditions (Achilles tendonitis, Baker's cyst, shifting skeletal structure due to extremely pronated ankles), prevented me from bending at the knee. I noticed that I could feel the chi energy almost as strongly when doing Lift Chi Up Pour Chi Down in the seated position as when I stood. Good news for all!

Here are some tips for you, arranged by category:

Modifying Physical Practice:

The first suggestion was mentioned in the paragraph above. Sitting in a chair is not limited to LCUPCD. Many of the medical qigong practices can be successfully accomplished in this fashion. For example: Chen chi, Lachi, Hip Rotation and Spinal Bone Marrow Rotation.

Wall squatting can be done in front of a chair, with arms crossed in front at elbows and hands gently pinching (opposite) ears. The chair is there for supporting tricky balance. There are some demos of this on the internet.

More about wall squatting: recently I began working with a Pilates Reformer (my gym offers these classes, as do many other gyms and physical therapy centers). By using the reformer machine, one can do the horizontal counterpart of a vertical wall squat.

I would also like to emphasize here that after several early gung-ho maniacal attempts at un-supported wall squats, I had to refrain for over a year. The point is that this practice was not a part of my early recovery routine, and yet the healing happened, and happened quickly.

It is also fine to perform part of a practice physically and to visualize movements that may be too painful or challenging, gradually attempting to add more of the physical component as the body strengthens and pain and/or fatigue subsides. Example: If one or both arms cannot reach above head, go as far as possible and then visualize the rest. Let your brain do the work for you till you can do more on your own.

Non-Physical Practice:

- Three gratitudes every evening.
- Inner/outer smile: Even a forced smile is more beneficial to body chemistry than not smiling or frowning.
- Use of Sound Healing and other meditational CDs can be substituted for physical practice if too fatigued, down with the flu, etc. It's more important to put in the time and visualize than to do nothing because of temporary physical limitations.
- Actively watching Wisdom Healing Qigong DVDs when fatigued or limited is beneficial also. Put your brain through the paces with visualization. When Michael Phelps was interviewed during the Summer Olympics, he was asked about his physical and mental preparation and he said he was doing physically better by working on visualizations every day.
- Become aware of negative self-talk, and for every negative self-thought, come up with at least two positive ones. Do the math: it's in your favor.

Flexibility (mind and body):

Oh, how we hate change, and oh how helpful it can be in eliminating all kinds of rigidity!

- Rearrange a desktop, pantry, bedroom.
- Practice walking backwards and side-ways in a safe, comfortable space.
- Practice walking forwards while holding a ruler horizontally across front of body. Pass it from one hand to the other in a continuous fluid motion around your body. I have seen several persons with Parkinson's, who couldn't otherwise, walk normally while doing this. Quite a revelation and harbinger of hope.

I offer you these little suggestions so you may try the ones that resonate for you and maybe then some that don't. It may not seem like much, but:

"In this life we cannot do great things. We can only do small things with great love."

- Mother Theresa.

I know I'm repeating here, but let's not forget this one.

Afterthoughts:

It is my hope that others who have tips will share them, and I would be pleased to use blog space for this.

Email me at bianca1738@aol.com or comment on my blog:

www.mettamorphix.com.

20

Sunnyside Down

"Of course there is no formula for success except perhaps an unconditional acceptance of life and what it brings."

- Arthur Rubinstein

I know that since I've shed Parkinson's my life is infinitely easier than it was before. Yet, lest people think my sunny side is always up, I wanted to expose the crack in the eggshell that allows the light to shine in. It's not like I healed from PD and instantly was granted the Rolls Royce of bodies. The work continues. Some muscle weakness is likely due to residual damage from years with the condition. Other difficulties existed long before to Parkinson's, and most likely contributed to it.

For many years prior to my awareness that I had PD, I was active and fit. Increasingly trimmer, too, possibly due to the weight loss many experience with this condition. Walking was my favorite form of exercise, and Marin County provides varieties of beautiful trails with spectacular views. The body/mind/spirit connection is there for the taking, and I especially enjoyed taking to the hills for the aerobics as well as the scenery.

Then, as Parkinson's progressed, I had to abandon the hillsides. A painful pull appeared in the shoulders every time I went uphill, and going down was a challenge to compromised balance (I never got the hang of those walking poles).

As my wonderful recovery began, with it came pain in legs and feet, particularly on the right side. Eventually when all PD symptoms had gone, and leg and foot pain and swelling continued, I figured something else had to be going on. Several diagnoses emerged: Achilles tendonitis, arthritic knee, Baker's cyst, pronated ankles due to fallen arches.

Why hadn't I felt these painful conditions earlier? Probably a combination of the denial that accompanies "powering through" along with being hyped on adrenalin. As dopamine took over and feelings emerged, I could feel the pain of decades of neglect. I say "neglect" because I knew from childhood that I had fallen arches and weak hamstrings. But why fix what didn't hurt, till it hurt?

I have often wondered how it is that I could feel so much pain with Parkinson's, yet not the pain in my legs and feet. There may be an answer in the in the research of Janice Walton-Hadlock who discovered in her case studies that people with Parkinson's were operating on adrenalin and not feeling their pain because of some early trauma which had shut down the dopamine system and diverted the energy flow, causing energy to run backwards, away from the brain. The fact that my leg issues began to emerge shortly after I began healing supports this theory. So not all avenues of pain were affected, just those on the related energy channel.

The time for me to address the situation is now, and it isn't easy! I'm at the gym on the recumbent bike, seated at the weight machines, and using the Pilates Reformer. All three types of exercise take place while seated or lying down, allowing me to keep weight off my legs and feet. Using my legs and feet in standing position would burn more calories, but I'm not there, not just yet.

Often now when I do Lift Chi Up Pour Chi Down, I keep a chair behind me in case the pain hits. Oh, I could power through it and look good, but why? How would that facilitate healing? Is that being kind to myself? So I continue to practice qigong without being my own stern taskmaster, as I was at the start. I remind myself that intent and attitude are far more important than form. I try not to succumb to the pressure I sometimes feel to be the perfect role model and inspiration, re-membering the words of Dr. Stanley Murad: "Be imperfect, live longer!"

Afterthoughts:

Still, I miss "my day in the hills" as the song goes, and work to return there. But I remind myself that this is not such a great loss, compared to all that I have gained.

21
Embracing the Shadow

"Human speech is like a cracked tin drum on which we hammer out tunes to make bears dance when we long to move the stars."

*- Gustave Flaubert, **Madame Bovary***

The citation above has always been my favorite quote, and inspired my only graffiti-writing experience, scrawled, in my youth, on the walls of the women's locker room at Jones Beach, NY. These words continue to humble me and make me strive for clarity in my tango with the keyboard.

In his latest book, "Language of Recovery," Dr. Robert Rodgers illustrates for us the subtleties of our everyday language and assists us as we navigate the lexicon of intention, exemplifying throughout how our choice of words can often sabotage our work on recovery. The type of recovery doesn't matter: Parkinson's, other chronic conditions, cancer, financial, any condition we wish to optimize. The words we select weigh in on either the positive or negative side of the scale, subtly affecting our sub-conscious, and therefore our conscious responses.

One of the many linguistic obstacles addressed in this book is the tendency to "fight" or "wage war" on whatever condition we are facing. My personal experience, which supports Rodgers' theory, began long before my Parkinson's ex-perience. When my younger son was diagnosed with autism, my initial response was a dualistic one: to separate him from his condition, and to attack the latter. Finding this impossible, I realized that unqualified love meant loving and accepting who he was as he was, in the moment, and working from there.

So when PD knocked on the door, I treated it as a visiting professor, hoping to learn from it as I did from autism. (Lest I leave you in a quandary, Justin is still autistic, but very high functioning. In his teens he received Auditory Integration Training and Sensory Integration Training; both treatments employed vibration, sound, and/or light, and greatly enhanced his quality of life. He has currently begun qigong energy healing and enjoys the calm and relief from stress.)

I was fortunate to have seen what could have been a tragic condition (neurologists suggested Justin be institutionalized as an infant) reversed, by refusing to succumb to the language of defeat. Justin, at age 36, lives nearby in a wonderful group home with a steady, caring staff, works part of each morning and socializes each afternoon as a piece of his specialized program. He enjoys all family functions and activities, travel, friendships, working on himself tirelessly, and has addressed numerous groups about his story as a member of "The Panel of Americans." A far cry from the infant who was diagnosed as blind, and most likely hearing impaired.

He taught me to keep positive language running in my head and to see him as the complete, though very quirky and original, person he is. This became a major advantage when I received my own diagnosis of PD.

I heard the neurologist tell me my condition was incurable, irreversible, and progressive. However, I brought my skepticism along to the altar of modern medicine. Why not? It followed me everywhere else. I remembered notes I had taken in a graduate class in the school of education many years before: "Education takes over where medicine leaves off." And I began to educate myself again, just as I had when I was given the bleak prognosis for my second son. In both cases, "the road less travelled" was a shortcut to fulfillment.

Afterthoughts:

Dr. Robert Rodgers continues to educate us and provide so many opportunities to learn about healing via his website and his books. (See Appendix)

Besides raising our awareness of how we can inadvertently wage war on ourselves when we "battle" a condition, Rodgers provides many other useful strategies. This is done in a friendly, interactive, workbook style. A deceptively easy read presenting some intense, life-changing work. Easily affordable online or in paperback. Haola!

To order *Language of Recovery* go to: www.languageofrecovery.us

22
Crybaby

"To weep is to make less the depth of grief."

- William Shakespeare

Last week I had composed a chirpy cheery holiday poem, and was ready to post it when the news of Sandy Hook broke out. I realize we have all been indelibly moved by this tragedy, and have tucked away the poem, perhaps for next year. Since then, like all of us, I have been attempting to process (inadequate word) this unspeakable tragedy. As a teacher, grandparent of young children, and mother to a kind and beautiful being on the autism spectrum, I found grief everywhere I turned.

There is often enough depression surrounding chronic health conditions, I don't want to possibly add to this; yet I find the need to remain authentic, as I think my own vulnerability is a gift I can share with you. My current position is to recall what it was like when I had

Parkinson's, and to reflect on the changes I perceive now, with the hope that this knowledge will prove useful to my readers. Thus the title: "Crybaby."

Tears flowed easily in early childhood, and they were not always induced by sadness. I remember the Christmas I received the dancing doll, table and chair set, and stuffed Bambi - I was so overwhelmed I began to cry. Then, of course, there were those other times - the conflicts with childhood friends that also brought on the waterworks. I cried early and often. This was not a diva strategy; the tears were heartfelt. Nevertheless, they must have made others uncomfortable.

The message I received, from youngsters and adults alike, was to "Stop it!", "Toughen up!", and to "Don't be such a crybaby!" and I followed the advice, figuring that there was something "wrong" with me I had to fix. As a young adult, I liked it when I sheared off my long locks - feeling that big brown eyes already had me looking too sensitive and vulnerable, that perhaps the tailored hairstyle would help me look tougher.

And it didn't stop there. Strong verbal skills and the sometimes "New York Jungle" fed my survival instincts and facility with sarcasm. I could easily engage anyone on the verbal battle-field. The "crybaby" had been transformed to a winner of sorts, or was she?

It has only been since my recent recovery from Parkinson's Disease that I find myself crying easily again, and surprised and grateful for the return of this necessary release. For years I suffered from lachrymose constipation, wanting to cry and being unable. When a dear friend died about seven years ago, the well remained dry for many months. Only at her memorial, with the aid of eulogies, music, mutual friends and memories, was I able to let go a bit. So during this last week, when I felt the waves of grief and accompanying tears as I thought of those families in Newtown, I welcomed the catharsis and viewed it as necessary and healthy, even if perhaps "inconvenient."

That was Step One. Step Two involved over-coming the helplessness one feels in the aftermath of such a senseless and horrific act. There is the urge to "do something" - but what? So I am working my way through Ann Curry's suggested 26 Acts of Kindness, perhaps even going for 28. I know from personal experience that love, though it does not control, can heal and bind. For me, it has become the only path. To quote Martin Luther King, Jr.: "I have decided to stick with love. Hate is too great a burden to bear."

I am also grateful. The reading I did when my son Justin was little suggested that parents of a disabled child needed to mourn the loss of the normal child they had expected. I was never able to do this - perhaps for some of the reasons shared above, but more likely because Justin and his brother, barely 18 months older, kept me so busy. After Sandy Hook, I realized how lucky I am and how wasted that grief would have been. I have my child, now an adult and a sweet, fun companion. Yes, he still keeps me challenged, but I see that as an opportunity for growth. No need for mourning on his account.

Further along that vein, no matter what the political affiliation, I think we can all find positive motivation in the words of President Barack Obama: "Let us find the strength to carry on, and make our country worthy of their memory." I suggest this is a way for all of us, worldwide, to welcome this new age and help shape our interwoven future.

Afterthoughts:

Although the focus of this piece discussed sadness and tears, I have noticed that other emotions have also come out of hiding. It surprises me to find myself chuckling aloud sometimes when watching TV: "Big Bang Theory" and "Too Cute: Puppies and Kittens" usually does the trick. Also, I can often feel a smile stretching across my face as I meditate. The benefits of this daily practice are exponential.

Conclusion

When I retired from teaching in 2008, I was too fatigued to plan anything for the future. Some who knew me asked if I would write, since I had originally been an English major and loved teaching writing and editing for others. Truthfully, I felt my muse had gradually deserted me. The well was dry. Yet, having the need for a creative outlet, I enrolled in an art class at the local community college, and after a few sessions, dropped out. I couldn't manage carrying all the necessary materials to class, due to extreme pain and stiffness. And once in class, the back pain from bending over my portfolio became distracting and prohibitive. Ever the optimist, I had hoped to replace the written word with the visual, telling myself that as my tremor intensified my work would become more original. So being an art class drop-out was a difficult experience. What next?

Now, a handful of years later, I sit at the keyboard, inspired. I hope that I am offering something of value to at least a few others. If not, I have at least realized an item on my bucket list that I thought I had to let go. *Reboot and Rejoice* is a dream materialized. In qigong we speak of the form and the formless. I am grateful that this nebulous idea of authoring a book, carried along from childhood, has been realized in material form. The lessons along the way have been enlightening, and I trust they will continue. I am grateful for all the people and experiences that have crossed my path since my recovery. I look forward to many new challenges and adventures. I take to heart the words of Pema Chodron:

"Whatever you are doing, take the attitude of wanting it directly or indirectly to benefit others. Take the attitude of wanting it to increase your experience of kinship with your fellow beings."

- Always Maintain a Joyful Mind,

www.pemachodronfoundation.org/store/buy-books/

May you walk in the way of the light.

Bianca

Appendix

Below is an alphabetical listing of the authors, books, quotes, websites, and other materials used or mentioned directly or indirectly in *Reboot and Rejoice* or works that I think would be of interest to anyone who wishes to travel a path of healing that resembles my own:

Shawn Achor, *The Happiness Advantage*

Eben Alexander III, M.D., *Proof of Heaven*

Pema Chodren, *Comfortable with Uncertainty: 108 Teachings on Cultivating Fearlessness and Compassion*

Deepak Chopra, M.D. and Rudolph E. Tanzi, Ph.D, Joseph P. and Rose Kennedy Professor of Neurology, Harvard Medical School, *SUPERBRAIN Unleashing the Explosive Power of Your Mind to Maximize Health, Happiness and Spiritual Well-Being*

John Coleman, ND, *STOP PARKIN' and START LIVIN': Reversing the Symptoms of Parkinson's Disease*

Joe Dispenza, D.C., *Evolve your Brain The Science of Changing Your Mind*

Randy Eady, www.Hollywoodhealingcenter.org

Duane Elgin, *The Living Universe*

Taro Gold, *OPEN YOUR MIND,OPEN YOUR LIFE A Little Book of Eastern Wisdom*

Amit Goswami, Ph.D., *THE QUANTUM DOCTOR: A Quantum Physicist Explains the Healing Power of Integral Medicine*

www.gratefulness.org

A network for grateful living

www.gratitudetwentyfourseven.com

Mingtong Gu, *WISDOM HEALING (Zhineng Qigong)*

www.chicenter.com

David R. Hawkins, *Power vs. Force: The Hidden Determinants of Human Behavior.*

www.healingquest.tv

Roger Jahnke, *The Healing Promise of Qi*

Suzanne Jonas,
www.innerharmonyhealthcenter.com

Judith Lynne,
www.PartneringwithParkinsons.com
www.HarmonicHealing.com

Dr. Robert Rodgers, numerous publications, radio broadcasts and events about PD

www.parkinsonsrecovery.com

www.blogtalkradio.com/parkinsons-recovery

Jo Ryan, *Go For It! Inspiring Words of Determination*

Spirit Rock Meditation Center: www.spiritrock.org

Janice Walton-Hadlock, *ALMOST ICARUS or Recovering from Parkinson's Disease: Understanding Its Cause and Mastering Effective Treatment*

Kobi Yamada, *LIVE GOOD*

90275540R00089

Made in the USA
San Bernardino, CA
08 October 2018